SUFFER

pg 45
attend to
our duty
more than
our deliverance

WHEN CHRISTIANS
SUFFER

Thomas Case

Edited
by
Richard Rushing

THE BANNER OF TRUTH TRUST

THE BANNER OF TRUTH TRUST
3 Murrayfield Road, Edinburgh EH12 6EL, UK
P.O. Box 621, Carlisle, PA 17013, USA

*

First Published as *A Treatise of Affliction* (1652)
© Richard Rushing 2009

ISBN-13: 978 1 84871 042 9

*

Typeset in 10.5 / 13.5 pt Adobe Caslon Pro
at the Banner of Truth Trust, Edinburgh

Printed in the USA by
Versa Press, Inc.,
East Peoria, IL

This version of Thomas Case's *Treatise of Affliction* is
drawn from his *Select Works* (Religious Tract Society:
London, 1836) and has been edited by Richard Rushing.

Introductory Letter
by
Thomas Manton
to
Thomas Case

I thank you for your thoughts concerning afflictions. I was pleased to drink from this fountain, and the half was not told me. To treat of afflictions when we ourselves flourish and abound in ease and plenty is more like the orator than the preacher, and the brain than the heart. It seems that when you went into prison, the Spirit of God went into prison with you. When you were shut up to others, you still were open to the visits and free breathings of his grace. A prison cannot restrain the freedom of his operations. It would be a prison for sure to be shut up also from fellowship with the Holy Spirit. I begin to see the truth in Tertullian's discourse to the martyrs:

> You went out of prison when you went into it, and were but sequestered from the world that you might converse with God; the greatest prisoners and the most guilty are those that are at large, darkened with ignorance, chained with lusts, committed not by the proconsul, but God.

Sir, I could even envy your prison comforts, and the sweet opportunities of a religious privacy. We that are abroad are harassed and worn out with constant public labours, and can seldom retire from the distraction of business for such free converse with God and our own souls. But we are not to choose our own portion; crosses will come soon enough without wishing for them, and if we were wise we might take an advantage of every condition.

Good sir, be persuaded to publish these discourses: the subject is useful, and your manner of handling it warm and affectionate. Do not deprive the world of the comfort of your experiences. Certainly my heart is not one of the tenderest, yet if heart answers to heart, I can easily foresee much success and that you will not repent of the publication. The Lord bless your endeavours in the gospel of his dear Son. I am, sir, yours in all Christian observance,

THOMAS MANTON.

INTRODUCTION

The discourse before you contains God's counsel and comfort to the generation of his sufferers.

We are great strangers to the cross, and when we suffer we either despise the chastisement of the Lord or we faint when we are rebuked by him. If the affliction is in measure we are apt to despise it and considerate it not worth taking notice of. But if the rod fetches blood, presently it is intolerable, and we begin to faint, crying out in our passion: 'Was ever sorrow like my sorrow?' But God's rod and God's love may stand together! Providence has so ordered that whosoever will follow the Lord fully like Caleb (*Num.* 14:24) will be exposed to the world's hatred, but the glorious Spirit will rest upon them (*1 Pet.* 4:14).

Discourses on affliction can never be out of season. In the following leaves are some prison thoughts. If I have not written what I have actually found, I bless God, I have written what I have sought. I must confess with holy Paul, 'Brothers, I do not consider that I have made it my own. But one thing I do: forgetting what lies behind and straining forward to what lies ahead, I press on toward the goal for the prize of the upward call of God in Christ Jesus' (*Phil.* 3:13-14). God has taught me something of the doctrine we are considering, if he would be pleased to teach me to put it into practice. God has in some measure shown me the benefits gained by afflictions, if he would also teach me how to gain it. I should with Moses account my sufferings 'greater riches than the treasures of Egypt' (*Heb.* 11:26). The discovery is sweet if my heart does not deceive me, and the possession is infinitely precious.

My prayers accompany these papers, that God who quickens the dead, and calls things that are not into being, might be pleased to make these broken expressions answer the aim.

THOMAS CASE

BLESSED IS THE MAN WHOM
YOU DISCIPLINE, O LORD,
AND WHOM YOU TEACH OUT
OF YOUR LAW

Psalm 94:12

I shall take discipline here in the utmost latitude, for all kinds and degrees of sufferings, whether from God, or man, or Satan. Whether sufferings for sin, or sufferings for righteousness sake.

I.

Twenty-one Lessons which God Usually Teaches His People in a Suffering Condition

(1.) The first lesson God teaches us by affliction is to *have compassion for those who are in a suffering condition.*

We are prone to be insensitive when we are at ease in Zion! Partly out of the delicacy of self-love which makes us unwilling to sour our own sweet blessings with the bitter taste of a strangers' afflictions. Upon this very account God brings a variety of afflictions and sorrows upon his own children. He suffers them to be plundered, banished, imprisoned, or reduced to great extremities, that by their own experience they may learn to draw out their souls to the hungry, and to be able to say within themselves, I know the heart of the afflicted soul; I know what it is to be plundered, starved, or cast into prison. 'Therefore he had to be made like his brothers in every respect, so that he might become a merciful and faithful high priest in the service of God, to make propitiation for the sins of the people' (*Heb.* 2:17).

(2.) Through sufferings God teaches us to *prize our outward mercies and comforts more, and yet to dote upon them less.* We need to be more thankful for them, and yet to be less ensnared by them. We can undervalue our mercies even while we glut ourselves with them! Behold, while men fill themselves with the mercies of God, they can neglect the God of their mercies.

When God is most liberal in remembering us, we are most ungrateful to forget God.

To enable us to put a true value on the mercies that our foolish, unthankful hearts delight in, God often cuts us short that we may learn to prize them by want. Thus the prodigal, while yet at home could despise the rich and well furnished table of his father, yet when God sent him to school in the swine trough he could value the bread that the servants ate! O, but let us be locked up awhile, removed from our dearest enjoyments, then the sight of a friend through an iron grate will be sweet and precious! Months and years of arbitrary enjoyments are past through, and we scarcely sit down to reflect seriously about our mercies. Seldom do we spread them before the Lord in prayer and thankfulness! In famine the very gleanings of our comforts are better than the whole vintage in the years of plenty. So God teaches us to prize our mercies by affliction and to use them in moderation. By feeding us sparingly, God abates and slackens the inordinate appetite. He takes off our hearts from indulgences in a suffering condition by discovering richer and purer satisfactions in Jesus Christ. The voice of the rod is, 'O taste and see how good the LORD is!'

(3.) A third lesson God teaches by his chastisements is *self-denial and obedient submission to the will of God*.

In prosperity we are full of our own will, and usually we give God counsel when God looks for obedience. We tell God how it might have been better, and we dispute

Thomas Case on Affliction 17

our cross when we should take it up. But bearing a little we learn to bear more. Folly is bound up in the heart of God's children as well as our own, and the rod of correction drives it far from them (*Prov.* 22:15). God fetches out the stubbornness and perverseness of our spirits by the discipline of the rod.

The bullock unaccustomed to the yoke is very impatient under the hand of the husbandman, but after he is accustomed to labour, he willingly puts his neck under the yoke. So it is with Christians, after a while the yoke of affliction begins to be well settled, and by much bearing we learn to bear it with quietness.

No one murmurs so much at sufferings as they who have suffered the least, and on the contrary we see many times that they who are the most patient have the heaviest burden upon their backs.

God works out by degrees the delicacy of spirit that we contract in our prosperity. Mercy makes us tender. At first, chastisement seems very bitter, but afterwards it yields the peaceable fruits of righteousness.

I shall not be a loser by my sufferings. One way or the other, God works his children into a sweet obedient frame by their suffering. Even Christ himself, the Son of God by nature learned obedience by the things that he suffered! (*Heb.* 5:8). By suffering God's will, we learn to do God's will. God has no such obedient children as those whom he nurtures in the school of affliction. At length God brings all his scholars to subscribe, What God wills, when God wills, how God wills; thy will be done on earth, as it is in heaven. A blessed lesson!

(4.) A fourth lesson or design in affliction is *humility and meekness of spirit.*

God led Israel forty years in the wilderness to humble them. Pride is a disease that naturally runs in our veins, and it is nourished by ease and prosperity. To tame this pride of spirit God takes him into the house of correction, and puts his feet in the stocks, and there teaches him to know himself (*Deut.* 8:3). A man by trouble comes to know his own heart which in prosperity he was a stranger to. He now sees the weakness of his grace, and the strength of his corruption, and this lays him in the dust; 'O wretch that I am!' Truly when a man has learned this lesson, he is not far from deliverance!

(5.) God also uses affliction to *reveal unknown corruptions in the hearts of his people.*

He reveals in the heart what pride, what impatience, what unbelief, what idolatry, what distrust of God, what murmuring, and what unthankfulness abides there that you never took notice of! Sin lies very close and deep and is not easily discerned until the fire of affliction comes and makes a separation of the precious from the vile. The furnace discovers the dross that lay hidden before. I could not have believed the world had so much interest in my heart and Christ so little. I did not realize my faith was so weak and my fears so strong. Woe is me, what a heart I have!

Besides all this, in the hour of temptation God brings old sins to remembrance; 'In truth we are guilty concerning our brother, in that we saw the distress of his soul, when he begged us and we did not listen. That is why this distress has come upon us' (*Gen.* 42:21). The guilt came back twenty years after Joseph's brothers had sold Joseph into slavery!

Suffering times are times of bringing sin to mind. Captivity is a time of turning in upon ourselves, and bringing back to heart our doings which have not been good in God's sight. Affliction empties us of ourselves, and makes us fly to Jesus Christ for righteousness and strength.

In a word, God lets us see what is crooked that we may straighten it, what is weak that we may strengthen it, what is wanting that we may supply it, what is lame that it may not be turned out of the way, but that it may rather be healed.

(6.) The school of affliction *teaches us to pray*.

He that has never prayed before will pray in affliction. 'So the captain came and said to him, "What do you mean, you sleeper? Arise, call out to your god!"' (*Jon.* 1:6).

Affliction causes men to pray more frequently. God's people are vessels full of the spirit of prayer, and God draws it out by affliction.

Alas, it is sad to consider that in our peace and tranquillity, we pray carelessly by fits and starts many times. We suffer every trifle to come and knock out prayer, but affliction keeps us on our knees.

He also teaches us in affliction to pray more fervently. Even Christ being in agony prayed more earnestly. Truly Christians, the prayers you are content with in the days of your peace and prosperity will not serve your turn in the hour of temptation. When you call to mind your short, slight, cold, dead, sleepy, formal devotion, you will be ashamed of them, and stir up your heart to take hold of God. For this very end God sends his people into captivity that he may draw out the spirit of prayer which they have allowed to lie dead within them.

(7.) Correction also brings the children of promise into *more acquaintance with the word of God*.

David was sent into the school of affliction to learn the statutes of God. Through correction the people of God learn to read the word more abundantly.

It is our duty at all times to study the word, and to let it dwell richly in us (*Col.*

3:16). (Outward distractions) and distempers many times cause the of God to be strangers to their Bibles. They suffer diversions to interpose between the word and their hearts. They pray carelessly, and they read carelessly, and allow their Bibles to be laid aside while they are taken up with entertainments in the world. God is forced to deal with them as we do with our children, to whip them to their books by the rod of correction.

Affliction also causes believers to understand the word more clearly. We would never understand some Scriptures had not God sent us into the school of affliction. It enables one to bring God's word and God's work together.

Affliction makes them relish the word more sweetly. In prosperity many times we suffer the luscious contentments of the world to remove our taste for the word. When God has kept them fasting from the world's dainties, the afflicted cries 'How sweet are your words to my taste!' The word is never so sweet as when the world is most bitter.

● Blessed be God for the correction that sweetens the word to us!

(8.) God by bringing his people into trouble teaches them *the necessity of full assurance of heaven and happiness*.

Alas, with what easy and slight evidences are we often satisfied with in times of prosperity when the candle of the Almighty shines in our tabernacles and peace and quiet is all around us! In the hour of temptation, fig leaves will cover nakedness no longer. Nothing will serve the turn but what will be able to stand before God and endure the trial of fire in the day of Christ. In that day one clear and unquestionable evidence of interest in Christ, and the love of God, will be worth ten thousand worlds. Shadows and appearances of grace will vanish before the searcher of hearts. Thunder-claps of his righteous judgments will awaken the vain creature out of foolish dreams in which if they should die they would be undone forever!

Let us be urging and pressing this question upon our own souls: Will this faith save me when I come to stand before the throne of the Lamb? Will this love give me boldness in the day of judgment? Will this evidence serve my turn when I come to die? Oh Christians, let us be afraid to lie down with the evidence in our beds that we dare not lie down with in our graves.

(9.) In times of trouble God teaches us to see *what an evil thing it is to grieve the Holy Spirit of God.*

When we are in the bitterness of our spirits and in need of comfort, we begin to call to mind how often we have grieved the Spirit. He is our Comforter, and has sealed us unto the day of redemption. In the hour of temptation I say: Ah, I am truly guilty concerning the tender Spirit of grace and comfort. I would not listen when he told me not to do this abominable thing. I have neglected his warnings and despised his counsels. I have undervalued his comforts and counted them a small thing. How just it is now if the Spirit should withdraw!

He should despise my sorrows, and laugh at my tears. It is well if the Lord shall be pleased to bring my soul out of trouble, and to revive my fainting spirit with his sweet consolation. I hope I shall carry myself, for the future, more obediently to the counsels and rebukes of Jesus Christ in my soul, and hearken to the least whisperings of the Spirit of grace.

(10.) Through chastisements, *God draws the soul into sweet and near communion with himself.*

Outward prosperity is a great obstruction to our communion with God; partly because we let out our affections to earthly things, and suffer the world to come in between God and our hearts. God's people offend most in their lawful comforts because the snare is not so visible as in grosser sins. While our hearts are warmed with prosperity we think many times that small sins can do no great harm, but this is a great deception.

The least sin has the nature of sin in it just as the least drop of poison is poison. In smaller sins there is greater contempt for God since we offend him for a trifle, as we count it, and venture his displeasure for a little sensual satisfaction. Great sins deeply wound the conscience and make the soul go bleeding to the throne of grace to mourn and lament, seeking rest for the soul by a fresh sprinkling of the blood of Christ and to recover peace and communion with God. Small sins are swallowed in silence with less regret and unknowingly alienate and estrange the heart from Jesus Christ.

Affliction sanctified deadens the heart to the world and awakens and makes the conscience tender towards sin. Like Augustine: 'Lord, you have made my heart for you, and it is restless until it can rest in you; Return unto your rest O my soul.'

When we through prosperity neglect Christ and are too familiar with strangers, what a gracious condescension it is in God to send us to the house of correction, and there by the discipline of the rod correct and work out the flesh and make us prepared for his presence. Then he takes us into sweet communion with himself again!

(11.) God *increases our grace* through affliction.

Sometimes the soul finds faith to be alive in a suffering condition. The same furnace of affliction where God tries our faith also refines it, purifies it and makes it live again!

The purest acts of faith are put forth in the dark! Faith is at its greatest strength when it cannot see, for it has nothing to stay itself upon but God. Man must first see the insufficiency of what he sees before he can believe in the all sufficiency of him that is invisible. It is harder to live by faith in abundance than in want. The soul is a step nearer living upon God when it has nothing to live upon but God. Faith's triumph lies in the midst of despair. God teaches us in affliction the necessity and excellence of a life of faith. Where sense ends, faith begins. When God pulls away the bulrushes of creature supports, the soul must either sink or swim.

God teaches this lesson by the uncertainty of secondary causes. A little hope today—and tomorrow reduced to despair. Good news today—and bad news tomorrow. O the ebbs and flows of all earthly hopes! One gives comfort, and another terror. A sick man hopes today for recovery, and then tomorrow he is at the point of death. What a heart-rending life is a life of sense! It is a life worse than death itself; to be tossed between hope and fear and to be baffled to and fro between the 'maybes' of secondary causes. God teaches us the necessity of a life of faith through these earthly disappointments. O bitter disappointments with no faith to support it!

Faith is never disappointed. God is always better than our expectations (2 *Tim.* 4:17). He only lives an unchangeable life that by faith can live in an unchangeable God.

Often we trust totally in the earthly knowing no other life but sense and reason. We seek to patch up a life between faith and sense which is not a life of faith at all. We do not live at all by faith if we do not live all by faith! Though we use means, we must trust God and trust him solely.

To bring us to this, God allows us to become tired of secondary causes and turn to Christ. We never resolve exclusively for God until with the prodigal we are whipped home stark naked to our father's house. There is no help in the best of men. Alas, he is but a little breathing clay. Trust in God is the only way that is able to make a man happy. Can anything be too hard for a creating God? Men may prove unfaithful, but God will never prove unfaithful (*Heb.* 10:23). The soul that comes to see the sweetness and excellence of a life of faith, will be kept in perfect peace since his mind is stayed on God. He truly lives indeed that lives in him who is Eternal!

A life of faith is a secure life, the only safe life. How secure is the one who lives behind the shelter of impregnable fortifications! Trust in the Lord forever, for in the Lord Jehovah is everlasting strength. Ages pass away one after another, but the Rock abides, and abides forever. In the Lord is everlasting strength. O the security of a life of faith!

A life of faith is as sweet as it is safe. Is it not a sweet thing to draw water from the fountain? 'You will keep in him in perfect peace, whose mind is stayed on you, because he trusts in you' (*Isa.* 26:3). Peace, peace; that is, multiplied peace; pure unmixed peace, constant and everlasting peace is the portion of him that lives by faith, unless sense and reason break in to disquiet it. In faith one lives in a most sweet and immutable serenity.

A life of faith is also an easy life. There is support that supersedes all cares (*Phil.* 4:6). Faith leaves a believer nothing to do but to pray and give thanks; to pray for what he wants, and to give thanks for what he has. It is true that believers must labour and travail in the use of means, as well as the rest of the sons of Adam, but O the thorn, the sting, which the sin of man and the curse of God has thrust in all of our labours of care and distraction, is pulled out by faith.

Faith can live upon God when there is famine upon the whole creation. The peace of God is like a court guard to fence the heart from all surprises of fear and trouble (*Phil.* 4:7). As faith can enjoy God in all things in the greatest of abundance, so she can enjoy all things in God in the deepest want.

The life of faith is an honourable and excellent life. And we experience it through our sufferings! God calls us out of the world and takes us to himself. He reveals by degrees the mystery and privilege of living upon him alone! God leads us away from self-confidence and teaches us to trust him more and ourselves less. Naturally we are prone to entertain and nourish high views of our own strength and of our own wisdom. In our prosperity we think ourselves able to carry any cross. We fancy ourselves strong enough to carry away even Samson's gates upon our shoulders. But when the hour of temptation comes we find that we are like other men and are ready to sink with Peter.

Usually suffering before it comes is like a mountain at a great distance, which seems so small that we think we could almost stride over it. But the nearer it approaches it appears insurmountable. Suppose a man would risk the scratching of his flesh to break through a hedge to save his life. Yet if God had taken away the hedge and built a wall instead, a wall so high that you could not clamber over it, a wall so thick that you could not dig through it, then the man in his affliction who thinks he can make it through by his own art and cunning will find his escape impossible without an immediate rescue by the arm of omnipotence.

Paul was brought into such a great straight and was at 'wits' end' (*2 Cor.* 1:8-9). But God had a plot in it, a design upon Paul; that he should not trust in himself, but in God that raises the dead. Paul was given a thorn in the flesh to protect him from self-confidence (*2 Cor.* 12:7).

God can raise the dead, and conquer the greatest difficulty. He that can put life into dead men can put life into dead hopes and raise up our expectations out of the very grave of despair. God that can put life into dead bones, is able to put life into a dead faith! Even those who have been given the largest proportions of faith and courage are suffered to languish under fears and to despair under insurmountable difficulties so they can recover holy confidence in God. We are proud creatures, full of self-confidence and so God by strange and unexpected providences hedges up our way with thorns, brings us to despair even of life, bereaves us of counsel, deprives us of all our own devises, brings us under the very sentence of death that we might not trust in ourselves, but in God who raises the dead. He overturns us by despair. He shows us what babes and fools we are in ourselves, that in all our future hazards and fears we might know nothing but God!

(12.) By affliction *God makes himself known unto his people.*

We discover more of God through afflictions than by many sermons. In the word we hear of God, but in affliction we see him.

Prosperity is the nurse of atheism. Understanding is clouded with the streams of lust in a prosperous estate. Men grow to be like brutes, and the reverence and sense of God is little by little defaced. By affliction the soul is gradually taken away from sense-pleasing objects, and the force of worldly allurements to be more capable of divine illumination. Truly the very godly themselves are exceedingly dark and low in their apprehensions of God! In the mean time by the divine strokes of vengeance, God makes the wicked know him to their cost, and by the rod of correction he makes his people to know him to their comfort.

God gives his people the most sensible experience of his attributes in their sufferings, his holiness, justice, faithfulness, mercy and all-sufficiency.

We experience in our sufferings the faithfulness of God the best. When our elder brother Esau is upon us, we can wrestle with the Jesus and not let him go until he blesses us!

In affliction we can press God for the return of our prayers. God cannot easily deny the prayer of an afflicted soul. If he does grant our requests, we can take notice of it and know our prayers when we see them again. 'I love the LORD, because he has heard my voice and my pleas for mercy. Because he inclined his ear to me, therefore I will call on him as long as I live' (*Psa.* 116:1-2).

God is never worse than his word. Affliction is a furnace to try the faith of God's people to test the faithfulness of God in his promises. Let a man cast in the promise a thousand times into the furnace, it will still come out with full weight. A man may see a heaven and earth upon a promise, and it will bear them up!

We also come to know God's mercy in our afflictions. It is of the Lord's mercies that we are not consumed. If my burning fever had been the burning lake; if my prison had been the bottomless pit; if my banishment from society with friends had been expulsion like Cain from the presence of God, and that forever, God would be righteous. It is never so bad with the people of God but it might have been worse. Anything on this side of hell is pure mercy! Mercy moderates our suffering and supports us in it. When David was sinking, God put his everlasting arms under him and held him up. Christ stretched forth his hand to sinking Peter. He often gives his refreshing mercy in our afflictions. He gives light and life to delight the soul. The soul hears of God's mercy in prosperity, but it tastes of God's mercy in affliction. O taste and see how good the Lord is!

We see God's all-sufficiency in our sufferings. We have seen what Pharaoh had done to Israel, and then what God had done to Pharaoh. The doubling of their burdens was the dissolving of their bondage. The same waters that were Israel's rocks, were Egypt's grave. As the tyrant cried, 'I will pursue, I will overtake, I will divide the spoil, I will destroy'; 'Not so', said God, 'You will sink in the mighty waters!' O sudden turn! There is Pharaoh drowned in the sea. Israel saw the great work of God on the Egyptians. God appears to his oppressed

Israel in the thick of their extremities. In prosperity God works, but we do not see him. Affliction opens our eyes and we see our dangers, then we see God's deliverances.

Instances are endless, but in suffering times, God makes his attributes visible. In the school of affliction God teaches lectures upon his attributes and expounds himself unto his people. So many times we come to know more of God experimentally by half a year's suffering than by many a year's sermons.

(13.) God teaches us in a suffering condition to *attend to our duty more than our deliverance*.

We need to seriously inquire what is the duty God desires for us under the present dispensation. 'Lord, what will you have me to do?' (*Acts* 9:6). There is no condition or trial in the world that does not give a man opportunity for the exercise of some special grace or the doing of some special duty. This is the work of a Christian in every new state and in every new trial— to mind what new duty God expects, and what new grace he is to exert and exercise.

To attend to deliverance only is self-love which is natural to man. Man in affliction desires for deliverance that the burden may be taken off. Men make more haste to get afflictions removed than to become sanctified. 'O', thinks a man, 'If God would heal me of this sickness, deliver me out of this distress, I would walk more closely with God, I would be more diligent in family duties, I would be more fruitful in my conversation, and I would do this and that.' It is good for a man in his afflictions to consider his ways and make new resolutions for better things if God shall give better times; yet this may be nothing more than a snare of the devil to gain time, a diversion to turn aside the heart from the present duty which God expects. God intends good and happiness to the soul by the present chastisement though leading the soul to his present duty.

We need to discern God's aim, and to find out the meaning of the present dispensation. Let us search and try our ways and turn again to the Lord. Paul studied more how to adorn the cross than to avoid it; how to render persecution amiable, and if he must suffer for Christ, yet that Christ might not suffer by him; that Christ might be exalted and the church edified (*Col.*

1:24). In suffering commit your souls to God as a faithful Creator in doing what is right (*1 Pet.* 4:19).

(14.) The next lesson God teaches us is that *it is a privilege to be in a suffering condition.*

In the school of affliction the Holy Spirit teaches us about the fruit and advantage of a suffering condition.

There is in every state of life a snare and a privilege. It is the folly and misery of man, that if left to himself, he willingly runs into the snare and misses the privilege. He is only able to add to his own misery and to make his condition worse than he finds it.

Those whom God loves, he teaches. He takes away creature comforts and by secret impressions of love upon the heart he teaches the soul to look out for restoration to a good condition (*Mark* 10:29-30). In a word, whatever the affliction is, it shall be the soul's gain.

In Romans 8:28 and Hebrews 12:12, God teaches his people that God's rod and God's love both go together. This is a sweet lesson indeed, it quiets the heart and supports the soul under its burden (*2 Cor.* 4:16). What we lose in our bodies we gain in our souls. What we lose in our estates we get in grace. Thus we can comfort ourselves in our deepest sorrows.

Those attending only to their afflictions aggravate their circumstances, sink their own spirits, vex their souls, and dishonour God by slandering God's dispensations and bringing up an evil report upon the

cross of Jesus Christ. God's suffering people taste peace and comfort for their soul
and so rejoice only in God, becoming more
than conquerors through him that loves us
(*Rom.* 8:37).

(15.) Another lesson God teaches in
affliction is *the one thing that is necessary*.

Christ taught Martha this. Affliction
reveals how much we are mistaken about
our must be's, and our necessaries. In our
health, strength, and liberty, we think this
thing must be done, and that thing must
be done. We think riches necessary, hon-
ours necessary, great estates necessary, large
portions for our children necessary and the
like. But in the day of adversity when death
looks us in the face, when God causes the
horror of the grave, the dread of the last

judgment, and the terrors of eternity to pass before us, then we can put our mouths in the dust, smite upon our breast and confess, 'O how have I been mistaken! O how I have fed upon ashes, and deceived my heart! How I have been deceived and made the unimportant the main thing and passed by the main thing!' In a word, Christ alone is the one thing necessary and all other things at best are the maybe's (*Phil.* 3:8-9).

O that Christians would be wise and not spend their money on that which is not bread, and labour for that which does not satisfy, but labour for faith to realize the unseen and spiritual things. They that do not learn this lesson in the school of the word, shall learn it in the school of affliction, if they belong to God.

(16.) *The redemption of time* is another lesson to be learned from God when he corrects.

In our tranquillity how many golden hours we throw down the stream that we are never to see again. The time may come when we would give rivers of oil, the wealth of both the Indies, and the mountains of precious stones, if they were ours, to recover one lost moment!

Who is there among us that knows how to value time and prize a day at a due rate? Most men study rather how to pass away their time than to redeem it. They waist precious hours as if they had more than they could tell what to do with. Our season is short, and we make it shorter. How sad a thing it is to hear men complain, 'O what shall we do to pass the time?' Alas, even the Lord's day, the purest and most refined part of time, how cheap and common it is in most men's eyes! But O, when trouble comes and danger comes, and death comes; when the sword is at the body, the pistol at the breast, the knife at the throat, death at the door, how precious would one of those despised hours be! Evil days cry with a loud voice in our ears: 'Redeem the time!' (*Eph.* 5:16). In life-threatening dangers, when God threatens, as it were, then we can think of redeeming the time for prayer, reading, meditation, and study. We then gather up the very fragments of time, that nothing may be lost. Then God teaches the soul the wisdom of redeeming the time.

We reckon upon years, many years yet to come, with many hours to make ready our accounts, but then the summons comes, and our time is gone, and our work yet to be begun. What a case we are in, to see the day spent and its work yet to do! It is a pity to loose anything that is so precious and so short.

(17.) Another lesson to be learned is to *rightly estimate the sufferings of Jesus Christ*.

In our prosperity we pass by the cross carelessly. At best we do but shake our heads a little. The reading of the story stirs up some compassion for him, but it is quickly gone. Then God pinches our flesh with some sore affliction, filling our bones with pain, setting us on fire with a burning fever, letting our feet be hurt in stocks, and then iron enters our souls. Let us be destitute, afflicted, tormented, then happily we sit down and look upon him whom we have pierced and begin to say within ourselves, Are the chips of the cross so heavy? What must have been the full cross itself that my Redeemer bore? Is the wrath of man so piercing? Is the buffeting of men so grievous? Is a burning fever so hot? Is a chain so heavy, a prison so loathsome, the sentence and execution of death so dreadful? O what was it for Christ to endure all the contradiction of sinners against himself, the rage of the devil, and the wrath of God!

Blessed be God my prison is not hell, my burnings are not unquenchable flames, my cup is not filled with wrath! Blessed be God for Jesus Christ through whom I am delivered from the wrath to come! Christ by his experience came to perfectly understand what his poor members suffer, so we by the remainders of his cross in some measure come to understand the sufferings of Christ.

(18.) The next lesson that God teaches by affliction is *to prize and long for heaven*.

In our prosperity, when the candle of God shines in our tabernacles, when we wash our steps in butter, and the rock pours us rivers of oil, we could sit down with this present world and say, 'It is good for us to be here!' While life is sweet, death is bitter, and heaven itself has no lustre while the world gives us her friendly entertainments. But when poverty and imprisonment, re-proach and persecution, sickness and sore diseases, pinch and vex our hearts with a variety of aggravations, we are not so fond of the earthly, and become content to entertain a parley with death and take heaven into our consideration.

God by discipline takes our hearts by degrees from this present world and makes us look homeward. He lessons the esteem of the world that we might discover the excellencies of heavenly comforts and draws out the desire of the soul to fully desire God's presence. Affliction shows the glories of heaven: to the weary it is rest; to the banished it is home; to the scorned it is glory; to the captive it is liberty; to the struggling soul it is conquest; to the conqueror it is a crown of life; to the hungry it is hidden manna; to the thirsty it is the fountain and waters of life, and rivers of pleasure; to the grieved soul it is fullness of joy; to the mourner it is pleasures for evermore; to the afflicted soul heaven cannot fail to be very precious.

Thomas Case on Affliction

(19.) In affliction God teaches us *the sinfulness of sin.*

Sin is always sinful, but in our prosperity we are not so aware of it. The dust of the world fills our eyes. We don't see clearly the evil that is in sin. In the sharp and bitter waters of affliction God washes out the dust and clears the eyes to discover sin.

God uses four glasses to reveal to the soul the evils of sin: 1. The glass of the law, 2. The blood of Christ, 3. Affliction and chastisements in this present world, and, 4. The torments of hell.

Of all these glasses, the blood of Christ most fully and perfectly declares the sinfulness that is in sin. The stain of sin can only be washed out with the blood of the Son of God. Though this is the purest glass, God often makes use of afflictions to reveal to the children of promise the great evil that is in sin. In the glass of affliction, God reveals a fivefold evil in sin.

(i.) *Sin is the cause of all evil.* Sin is the mother evil. Thank yourself for all the affliction that is upon you. Are you in captivity, in prison, in distress, &c? Thank your idolatries and adulteries by which you have forsaken the Lord your God. Thank yourself for all the misery that is upon you. Every man's heart may say to him, You are the cause for all this! Lust when it is conceived brings forth sin, and when sin is finished it will bring forth death (*James* 1:15). Sin is the child of lust, and the mother of death.

(ii.) *Sin is an evil in itself.* It is an evil and bitter thing. Sin does not only bring evil, it is evil. It not only works bitterness, it is bitterness. It has a bitter root and brings forth bitter fruit. God leads the sinner by affliction to take notice not only what sin does, but what sin is; it is evil!

(iii.) *Sin is an unmixed evil.* In the sorrow of affliction there is some good, for it has God as its author (*Amos* 3:6; *Rom.* 8:28; *Psa.* 119:71). But sin is a simple uncompounded evil for it has the devil for the author (*1 John* 3:8). The wages of sin is death (*Rom.* 6:23). Sin is evil all over.

(iv.) *Sin is an evil against God.* It is a departure from God. It is a twisted and multiplied evil. It is a departure from the fountain of life and glory. It is a contradiction to the will of God. There is more evil in the least sin than the greatest punishment, even hell itself. The hell that is in sin is worse than the hell that is prepared for sin.

(v.) *Sin has no justification*. God has led you by the way. He supported you with his everlasting arms. He was a guard to you, and a Father to provide for you. You lacked nothing, and yet you forsook the Lord (*Jer.* 2:17). Why this causeless apostasy and rebellion? The soul sins only because it will sin. Affliction is one of God's tribunals where the sinner is arraigned, convicted, and condemned. Truly in affliction sin is laid open before a man's eyes so he is forced to plead guilty. God sits as judge; conscience is witness, a thousand witnesses; sin the indictment; affliction both evidence and execution. Sooner or later the convinced soul sees sin a greater evil than affliction. Forgetting the affliction he begins to mourn only for sin.

(20.) In affliction God teaches us *the emptiness of earthly things.*

In our prosperity we hold and dote upon earthly things, the things and persons in this present world as if our happiness and comfort were bound up in them. Then in the day of adversity, God convinces us of our mistake by causing us to see the emptiness and vanity of all earthly contentments. We begin to find the world a gilded emptiness and mere nothing. The afflicted soul sees all flesh as grass and pleasure as the flowers of the field. It looks on the earthly as nothing. It is not what it seems; not what it promises; not what we expect and flatter ourselves with. Whatever a man makes his riches, whether friend, or wealth, they cannot profit or deliver you out of the hands of death or judgment. The soul finds by experience the unsuitableness and dissatisfaction for all these things. There is no comparison between the immortal soul and perishing contentments. If a man tries to swallow the wind it will as soon fill his hungry belly as creature-comforts will satisfy the spirit. In the hour of temptation the soul will say; 'Miserable comforters you all are, you physicians of no value.' The day of affliction is one of those days to cast away the idols of silver and gold!

(21.) In the day of affliction *God reveals to the soul the fullness of Jesus Christ.*

There is an infinite fullness in Jesus Christ. There never was a king anointed with such power. There was never a prophet with such wisdom. There was never a priest with such grace and righteousness. God did not give his Spirit by measure to him (*John* 3:34). It is infinite fullness which fills Jesus Christ as Mediator that we might of his fullness receive grace for grace. But we do not always have a capacity to receive or to see that fullness. The reason is that we fill ourselves so much with the world in our prosperity. We seek the pleasures and profits of the world, and have no room for Christ. Like at his birth, there was no room for him in the inn. The world glitters in our eyes and there is no beauty in him that we should desire him (*Isa.* 53:2). We are very prone to love the world and be satisfied in earthly things themselves instead of these leading us to be more fitted to walk with God. In this case, the greater our love of earthly things, the less our delight in Jesus Christ. This is our sin and folly that we do not fear the unlawful use of lawful things. We do not see the snare for us to be encouraged to love earthly things in such a way that is only due to God himself. This brings a great reproach to Jesus Christ.

But when God spreads sackcloth upon all the beauty and bravery of the earthly, and by some flashes of lightning strikes us blind to the world, then we can discover the beauty and excellence of Christ. It infinitely transcends all the beauty and excellence of the world. When the God of heaven has famished all our gods on earth, and has starved us of our creature-comforts, in any way whatsoever, then we can hunger after and taste the sweetness, the fullness, which is in Jesus Christ. O then, Christ is a King to govern, a Prophet to teach, and a Priest to save! How precious! Give me nothing but Christ or else I die! Truly God sees it absolutely necessary to exercise us with a severe discipline that he may endear Jesus Christ to our hearts and seclude us from the world that we may study and know deeper of his fullness.

II. The Nature or Properties of Divine teaching.

Everything that one might learn in affliction is not necessarily a blessing. Hardly any man under affliction does not learn something, but few are blessed by it. It matters more who is the teacher than what a man is taught. We must be taught of God for affliction to become a blessing. There are common teachings, which even the heathen and hypocrites have. The philosophers also have given excellent lectures upon affliction. But there is a special teaching that is proper and peculiar only to the children of promise. The teachings of God have a six-fold property.

(1.) *It is an inward teaching.*

Man may lead you unto truth, but only the Spirit of God can lead you into truth. Only he that has the key of David, that opens and no man shuts, and shuts and no man can open, can truly reveal truth to the inner man. Man may teach the brain, but only God can teach the heart. 'For God, who said, "Let light shine out of darkness", has shone in our hearts to give the light of the knowledge of the glory of God in the face of Jesus Christ' (2 *Cor.* 4:6). Man's light may shine into the head, but God's light shines into the heart. God has a throne in heaven, but his chair, his pulpit is in the heart.

(2.) *When God teaches it is clear and convincing.*

The Holy Spirit brings divine truths with such clear and convincing light that the soul sits down under it fully satisfied. God's teaching gives assurance and the soul sweetly and freely is able to acquiesce in the present truths. 'I know, O LORD, that your rules are righteous, and that in faithfulness you have afflicted me' (*Psa.* 119:75). 'Because our gospel came to you not only in word, but also in power and in the Holy Spirit and with full conviction. You know what kind of men we proved to be among you for your sake (*1 Thess.* 1:5).

(3.) *The third mark of Divine teaching is that it brings the soul to experience the teaching.*

Like David; 'It is good for me that I was afflicted, that I might learn your statutes (*Psa.* 119:71). Most only have the notion in their heads, and on their lips, but David knew by experience the good he had gained through affliction. He had learned more acquaintance with the word, more delight in the word, and more conformity to the word. He knew it more, loved it better, and was more transformed into the spirit of it than ever before. Paul said; 'I know whom I have believed' (*2 Tim.* 1:12). He had experienced God's faithfulness and his all sufficiency. He could trust his all with him. He was sure God would keep him safe until that day. Thus, those who are taught by God in affliction can speak experimentally, in one degree or other, of the gains and privileges of a suffering condition. They can speak experimentally of communion with God (*Psa.* 23). He can say; 'I have had a comfortable experience of God's upholding, counselling, comforting presence with me in my deepest desertion. By my sufferings I bless God I have learned more patience, humility, self-denial, &c. I have learned to be more sensitive to my brethren's sufferings, to sit looser to the world, to mind duty, and to trust safely with God, to prepare for death, and to provide for eternity. It has been good for me, I could not have been without this affliction!'

Common knowledge rests more in generals and propositions than in application. They that have been taught by God can say; 'As we have heard, so have we seen;

I have experienced the word upon my own heart, and set my seal that God is true!' (*John* 3:33).

(4.) *God's teaching is powerful teaching.*

After a man had received many truths in his understanding, the main work was yet to be accomplished. It needed to bring down the holy truths to action, to draw forth divine principles into practice. A natural man may know much, he may have a heap of truths in his understanding, but they all lay strengthless in the brain. He has no power to live the truths he knows.

Covenant-teachings convey strength as well as light. Yea, the best of men; Job, David, Jeremiah, Habakkuk, Peter, &c, staggered for a time, and then recovered by a powerful word from heaven. This is a privilege of the children of promise, that strength goes out from the covenant with the instruction. God taught us by such a word, a creating word, a word that gives strength as well as counsel. Mark this— not only does he teach me the way, but he teaches me to go the way; he not only teaches me his will, but teaches me to do his will!

(5.) *God's teachings are sweet and pleasant teachings.*

The Psalmist rolled the word and promises as sugar under the tongue. He got more sweetness from it then Samson did from his honeycomb (*Psa.* 119:102-103). Luther said, he would not live in paradise, if he must live without the word; but with the word he could live in hell itself. When

Christ teaches the heart, his fingers drop sweet smelling myrrh upon the handles of the lock (*Song of Sol.* 5:5). Saving teaching is sweet and delightful, but never sweeter than the word during affliction. The bitterness of adversity gives a sweet taste for the word. It heals the distempers of the spiritual palate, and cries out with Jeremiah in the prison: 'Your words were found, and I ate them, and your words became to me a joy and the delight of my heart, for I am called by your name, O LORD, God of hosts' (*Jer.* 15:16).

(6.) *God's teachings are abiding teachings.*
'But the anointing that you received from him abides in you' (*1 John* 2:27). Mere notional knowledge is fleeting and inconsistent, and leaves the soul uncertain.

Human teaching begets at best opinion not faith. They may be good words in trouble, but yield poor performance out of trouble. No sooner are they out of affliction but they fall again into their old trade of spiritual adultery against God. No sooner do their old hearts and their old temptations meet, but they embrace each other. They are like a broken bow. But David was taught by God, and was very careful to make good his vows as much as he was to make them. 'I will come into your house with burnt offerings; I will perform my vows to you, that which my lips uttered and my mouth promised when I was in trouble' (*Psa.* 66:13-14).

When we say God teaches inwardly, clearly, experimentally, powerfully, sweetly, abidingly, we are not to understand that God teaches all of these at first. He does not teach all the truth of his lessons at the first entrance into the school of affliction, at least not usually, for we dare not limit what God can do. The fruit of affliction is not gathered immediately. 'For the moment all discipline seems painful rather than pleasant, but later it yields the peaceful fruit of righteousness to those who have been trained by it' (*Heb.* 12:11). Teaching is the fruit of affliction and is not gathered immediately. It must have a ripening time.

Therefore, O discouraged soul, do not say that God does not teach you at all if he does not teach you all at once. God lets in the light be degrees. Usually he teaches his children as we teach ours, now a little and then a little (*Isa.* 28:10); something this week, and more next week; something by this affliction, and more by the next &c.

It should be an encouragement if God reveals to your soul the need of divine teaching and engages the heart in holy desires, and longing after it so that the afflicted soul can say in sincerity, 'My soul is consumed with longing for your rules at all times' (*Psa.* 119:20).

Also when we say that God teaches whom he chastens, it does not mean that he teaches all men alike. God has several classes in the school of affliction as well as in the school of his word. If God has not taught you as much as another, do not say he has not taught you at all. As one star differs from another in glory, so it is in the school of Christ. It is free grace that you are a star. Don't worry that it is not a star of the first magnitude. Even if God has not let in as much divine light as another might have, yet you are in God's school! With the view to grow, we should be aware of degrees of grace, but with regard to thankfulness and comfort we should consider that we are a part of grace.

When we say that God teaches powerfully and abidingly, it is not to be understood that through these teachings we arrive at an immutable evenness of spirit and are freed from all insurrections and disturbances from our corruption. Such a frame of soul is only the privilege of the glorified state when we will see God face to face. Then we will dwell in immutability to all eternity. On earth we are full, but then lacking. David had his sinkings, and Job had his impatient fits. We have heard of the patience of Job, yea and of his impatience too. Those taught of God may be moved, but not removed. Fall they may, but not fall away; fearfully, but not finally; terribly, but not totally.

Believers, however, can sense the least stir or whisper of corruption. It displeases them when they find things in their nature that are against the teachings of God. Luther when he found a distemper upon his spirit would never give over praying until he had prayed his heart into the frame he prayed for. We are able by virtue of the teachings of God to maintain an opposition against all the evil we find in our own spirits. Life for the believer is called a wrestling, and a warfare (*Eph.* 6:12). We gain ground over our fleshly opposition by degrees. Prayer brings in God, and God brings in strength. All is not done at first, but we are comforted that all should be done in God's time. I am not perfect, but I shall be perfected. 'And I am sure of this, that he who began a good work in you will bring it to completion at the day of Jesus Christ' (*Phil.* 1:6). We may not always be the same in temper and action, yet we are the same in purpose and design. Clouds of opposition may intercept and disturb sweet and constant communion with God sometimes, but we will eventually break through to recover God's presence again: 'My soul follows hard after you.' Paul was pressing after perfection when he could not overtake it (*Phil.* 3:12).

III. How the Instrument of Affliction Promotes the Teachings of God in the Soul.

One might ask; 'Might not God as well teach his people by sin as by affliction?' He might, and he does! (*Rom.* 8:28). 'All things' demand no exception to things working for our good. All things work, but all things do not work alike. Sin works for good, but it is by absolute omnipotence, by pure prerogative, for sin is properly the devil's work, and in its own natural tendency works merely to destruction. It is no thanks to sin that any good come of it; God beats Satan with his own weapons.

But affliction is a calamity of God's making (*Amos* 3:6). God has so tempered the nature of it and directs it by divine skill, to make it fit and disposed to serve and promote his own gracious designs in the children of promise. It is true there is the need of the arm of omnipotence to make chastisement have a saving influence upon the heart as the word or divine ordinances. These do not save by any intrinsic value or power of their own, but they are useful instruments to serve divine omnipotence unto profitable ends for his children. They are instruments as a saw is to cut or a wedge to cleave &c. The instrument can do nothing alone, but there is fitness in them to serve the hand of the workman.

There is a tendency in the rod as there is in the word to teach and instruct the children of God. Affliction prepares the heart and puts it into a disposition to embrace divine teachings. The hot furnace is God's work-room in which the most excellent vessels of honour are formed. Manasseh, Paul, the jailer, were all chosen in this fire; 'I have tried you in the furnace of affliction' (*Isa.* 48:10). Grace works in power. God speaks when we are most apt to hear. It comes in power, in keeping with the circumstances. How does God carry on this work through affliction?

(1.) *Through affliction God tears down the pride of man's heart.*

There is no greater obstruction to saving knowledge than pride and self-opinion. Man thinks he knows enough. Pride raises objections against the word, and disputes the commands when they should obey them. The heart of man stands as a mountain before the word, and cannot be moved until God comes with his instruments of affliction and knocks down those mountains, and then stands on level ground to talk with man. This pride of heart speaks loud in the wicked, and whispers audibly even in the godly. It is a folly bound up even in the hearts of God's children until the correction drives it out, and the pride is broken and cries, 'Lord, what will you have me to do?'

(2.) *Affliction is God's forge where he softens the iron heart.*

You cannot work with iron while it remains cold and hard. Put it into the fire, and make it red-hot there, and you may stamp upon it any figure or impression you please. Melted vessels are impressionable to any form. So it is with the heart of man. By nature it is cold and hard, and this is much increased by prosperity and the longsuffering of God toward sinners. The furnace makes the soul pliable to God's counsel, and sometimes God is forced to make the furnace heated seven-times hotter to work out the dross that renders men so resistant to the ministry of the word. When the earthly heart of man is so dry and hardened by the long sunshine of prosperity so that the plough of the spiritual husbandman cannot enter, God softens it with the showers of adversity that it might receive the immortal seed. The seed falls upon stony ground until God turns the heart of stone into a heart of flesh.

(3.) *Chastisement makes man more attentive of God.*

Prosperity in the world makes such a noise in a man's ears that God cannot be heard. God speaks again and again but man does not hear. He is so busy in the crowd of worldly affairs that God is not heeded.

In the godly themselves there is much unsettledness and giddiness of mind. Our thoughts are vain and scattered, the spirit is slippery and inconsistent. These are great impediments to our clear and full comprehensions of spiritual things.

God deals with man as a father with his child playing in the market place that will not listen or mind his father's call. He comes and takes him out of the noise of the tumult, carries him into his house, lays him upon his knee with the rod in his hand, and then the father can be heard. When Joab would not come to Absalom, he set his field on fire (*2 Sam.* 14:30). When we neglect God, he brings us to pay attention to him by affliction.

(4.) *Affliction is an eye-salve that opens our eyes to see the need and excellencies of divine teaching.*

We are then able to see our ignorance of God and his ways of divine administrations. Affliction draws out the heart into a humble, holy desire for God's divine teaching. God brings the heart into this frame to lie in the dust at God's feet and humbly seek his effectual instructions from heaven. And, when he has prepared the heart to pray, he will cause his ear to hear! (*Psa.* 10:17). When God has engaged the heart by mercy to seek saving instruction, in his faithfulness he will satisfy his creature and teach him in the way (*Psa.* 25:8).

IV. Information to Improve
the Point

(1.) *No man is blessed just because he is afflicted.*

Blows alone are not enough to effect a state of blessedness. Blows alone may break the neck sooner than the heart. It is very sad to consider that affliction is the best evidence that most men have for heaven. Because they suffer in this world they think they shall be freed from suffering in the world to come. They believe that since they have a hell here, they hope they shall escape hell hereafter. They hope they shall not have two hells.

Yes, poor deluded soul, you may have two hells if you do not have any better evidence for heaven! Cain had two hells, and Judas had two hells, and millions of reprobate men and women have two hells; one in this life, in torments of body and horror of conscience; and another in the life to come, in unquenchable fire.

The plagues and evils that are upon you may be but the beginnings of sorrows. Pain now in the body may be but a forerunner of torments hereafter in your soul. You may have a prison on earth and a dungeon in hell; you may now lack a crumb of bread, and hereafter a drop of water; you may now be the reproach of men, and hereafter the scorn of men and angels, and of God himself. Therefore be wise to salvation by working it out with fear and trembling (*Phil.* 2:12).

And note, though the Scriptures says that those whom the Lord loves he corrects, it does not say whoever receives correction is a son. Scripture ties chastening to sonship, but not sonship to chastening. Sons are chastened, but all that are chastened are not therefore, sons. Many are happy in affliction only when it is accompanied by the teaching of God! Chastening and affliction is an opportunity of mercy, and a maybe to happiness, but not by itself. It must be accompanied by instruction.

Do not lay more upon it than it will bear. It is an opportunity, improve it. It is no more, do not trust in it.

(2.) *As affliction, simply considered is not enough to make a man happy, so neither is it sufficient to conclude that a man under affliction is miserable.*

It may be a teaching affliction, and thus the man can be happy. When we look at others, we are prone to judge them wretched if they are under affliction. This was Job's friends mistake. Even God's own children sit down in affliction (especially if it is sore and lasting a long time), and conclude that God does not love them because he corrects them.

But I say, to establish this as a proper conclusion of unquestionable truth, namely, that God's love and God's rod may stand together. The truth is, my brethren, there is nothing that can make a man miserable but sin. The sting of sickness is sin. The sting of poverty is sin. The sting of imprisonment is sin, and so the rest. Take the sting of sin out, which is purchased by the blood of Christ, and they cannot hurt nor destroy in all God's holy mountain (*Isa.* 11:9).

Therefore let no children of God be rash to conclude hard things against themselves and to look for evidences of wrath where God has made none. Let Christians look beyond the affliction itself. Judge your estate by the word of God, and not by providence. Evidence of grace consists in inward impressions, not in outward dispensations.

(3.) *Deliverance out of trouble is not enough to make a man happy.*

Blessed is the man only if God also teaches! A man may get rid of the affliction, and yet miss the blessing. A man may leave his chains and his blessing behind him in prison. The fire of a fever may be extinguished, when the fire of hell is preparing for the sinner. It is good to be thankful for, but extremely dangerous to be contented with, a bare deliverance.

Prayers that are prayed in troubles are not best answered with deliverance, but with instruction. Christ offered up prayers with strong crying and tears, unto him that was able to save him from death, and he was heard (*Heb.* 5:7). How was he heard? Not in that, 'Save me from this hour' (*John* 12:27), but in this; 'Father, glorify your name' (verse 28). The best return of our prayers is that which works our good, though not according to our desires; when God does not answer in the letter but in the better. We are not a looser by our prayers.

When we have prayed, let us leave it unto God to determine the answer.

(4.) *If God has taught you as well as chastened you, you are a blessed man.*

It is sad when men come out of affliction the same as when they went in; when affliction leaves them as it found them; ignorant, proud, insensible of sin, uncaring about suffering brethren, worldly, impatient, unsavoury, a stranger to Christ, a stranger to their own hearts, and unconcerned about eternity. This, I say, is exceedingly sad. Yet it is much sadder when it may be said of a man like Ahaz, 'In the time of his distress he trespassed yet more against the LORD' (*2 Chron.* 28:22).

Christians, it is sad and dangerous beyond all expression when affliction only gives vent against the Lord, like oil to the fire. In such cases it is to be feared, the cup of affliction is a vial of wrath. The plagues of this life are nothing else but drops of that storm of fire and brimstone in which impenitent sinners shall be scorched and tormented for ever. Neither the word, nor rod, nor judgments, nor ordinances can stir them. They refuse to receive correction; they will not be taught. Men will give God a hearing, but are resolved on their own course. They are the same that they ever were. The swearer is a swearer still, and the drunkard is a drunkard still, and the unclean person is unclean still. A fearful sentence!

When teaching does not go along with correction, when men come out of the furnace and do not lose their dross, it is a sad indication of a reprobate spirit. Without a timely and serious reflection they are near unto cursing. O consider this, you who forget God lest he tear you in pieces and there be none to deliver (*Psa. 50:22*).

(5.) *Those whom the world accounts miserable may be blessed.*

The world judges merely by outward appearances, and therefore may easily be mistaken. They see the affliction that is upon the flesh, and from this conclude a man to be miserable, but they cannot discover the divine teaching that is upon the spirit that renders him incomparably blessed.

Men of the world are not competent judges of the estate and condition of God's children. A godly man's happiness or misery is not to be judged by the world's sense of feeling but by his own. His sense of happiness is inward and the standard of the world is outward, made up of sense and reason. The spiritual man can judge the condition of the world, but the world is unable to judge his condition because it is above their natural faculties. The natural man thinks the spiritual man under affliction to be miserable, but the spiritual man knows the natural man in the midst of his greatest abundance and finery to be miserable indeed. God's day is coming when things and persons shall be valued by another standard. Christ will judge not after the sight of the eyes, not as things as they appear to sense and reason, not after the hearing of the ears but with righteousness. He will judge things as they are and not as they appear.

(6.) *We can admire the wisdom, power, and goodness of God, who can make his people better by their sufferings.*

Who knows how to fetch oil out of the scorpion, or to extract gold out of clay! God can draw the richest wine out of gall and wormwood. He can turn the greatest evil of the body to the greatest good of the soul. He can turn the curse into a blessing. He can make the withered rod of affliction to bud, and to bring forth the peaceable fruits of righteousness.

Behold I show you a mystery: sin brought affliction into the world, and God makes affliction to carry sin out of the world. Persecution is but the pruning of Christ's vine. The almond tree is said to be made fruitful by driving nails into it and letting out a noxious gum that hinders the fruitfulness. God never intended more good to his children than when he seems to deal most severely with them. God would rather fetch blood, than lose a soul. He would rather break Ephraim's bones than to allow him to go on in the frowardness of his heart. Destroy the flesh that the spirit may be saved in the day of the Lord Jesus.

(7.) *A suffering condition is not so formidable a thing as flesh and blood represents it.*

It is ignorance and unbelief that slanders the dispensations of God and casts reproach upon the cross of Christ. O that the children of God in affliction, or entering upon sufferings, would sit down and dwell upon this consideration: the fruit and advantage which God knows how to bring out of all their sorrows, even the peaceable fruits of righteousness. This would keep them from uncomely despondency and dejection of spirit. 'For this cause we faint not', said the apostle (*2 Cor.* 4:16-18). Why? 'Because we do not look at the things that are seen, but at the things that are not seen'! The things that are not seen are the invisible fruit and advantage of our sufferings. This holds up the head, and keeps up the heart. He makes the soul not only to be patient, but to glory in tribulation (*Rom.* 5:3-5). The best way to counteract the temptation to discouragement is to find comfort in the blessings of affliction.

(8.) *Truly, God not only brings his children into the school of affliction, but many times keeps them there a long time.*

The rod may lie long, for months, for years, for many years together. Israel was seventy years in the house of correction at Babylon. They were four hundred years in the brick kilns of Egypt. History and experience will serve as illustrations without number. Hence you have the people of God so often crying their how-longs in their sufferings: 'But you, O LORD, how long?' (*Psa.* 6:3). 'How long will you forget me, O LORD? forever? How long will you hide your face from me? How long shall mine enemies be exalted over me?' (*Psa.* 13:1-2). When deliverance is near, they can't believe it! (*Acts.* 12:9).

What is the reason that God suffers affliction to lay so long upon the backs of his children? One reason is that they have lived long in sin. They have been long in sinning, and therefore God is long in correcting. God puts them to their how-longs, because they put God to his how-longs.

'How long will you refuse to keep my commandments and my laws? How long will this people provoke me?'

Another reason is that the work is not yet done. They do not receive instruction by their afflictions, or the affliction would quickly cease. God does not give a blow, nor draw one drop of blood more than necessary. 'In this you greatly rejoice, even though now for a little while, if necessary, you have been distressed by various trials' (*1 Pet.* 1:6). If there is heaviness, there is need for it. If the heaviness continues long, there is need of it. It is not to gratify our enemies that God keeps his people so long under their stripes, but to teach them. God does not afflict willingly (*Lam.* 3:33). He seeks to do them good in their latter end. The rod of correction drives out the folly that is in the heart. When this is done, their deliverance does not delay. God opens the prison doors and throws the rod into the fire. This is infinite mercy that we are not delivered until we are bettered. God does not cease chastening until we are willing to cease sinning!

(9.) *Consider what unteachable creatures we are by nature.*

We do not set our hearts for instruction until we are whipped to it by the rod of correction, and hardly then! Unless God multiplies stripes, the multiplying of precepts will do us no good. There must be stripe upon stripe, and affliction upon affliction, as well as line upon line, and precept upon precept, or else it is in vain. We would say that it is a very bad child that will be taught no longer than the rod is upon his back! But, such are we! We put God to it as it were, to study what methods and courses he will take with us.

(10.) *Contentment in affliction shows our love for the word of God.*

He that loves the word dearly, will for the word's sake love affliction. The whip, the rod, the prison, the wilderness, anything is precious that brings instruction with it.

Carnal people can be content to die in their ignorance as long as they can die in comfort. Gracious hearts do not think it a great thing to go to prison; even while the blood is running down their back, if they can be taught by it! O the difference that grace and nature make of the same dispensation! The treasure of instruction is

so precious that there is none too old, none
to wise, none too high, to be put into the
meanest school of tribulation on this side
of heaven.

V. Exhortation

(1.) *To those who are free from sufferings. If the Almighty shines in your tabernacle,
and your steps are washed in butter &c. how
can you prevent chastisement, and keep off the
strokes of divine displeasure?*

If you would prevent chastisement,
study well the teachings of the word. God
sends us into affliction because we have
not been proficient in the school of God's
word. We force God to turn us over to the
rod. Profit much by the teachings of Jesus.

Set your heart to all the truths and counsels of God revealed to you. Set your hearts to the lessons taught in the word.

Neglect forces God to send us into captivity. Remember those in prison as if bound with them. Learn to sympathize with all the people of God under any adversity whatsoever. Hide not your eyes, and do not shut up your heart of compassion from any in a suffering condition, or you may have to learn by experience what it is to be plundered, and what it is to lie in chains. Prize your creature comforts more, but don't over-indulge. Study self-denial and meekness of spirit. Labour to discover the hidden corruption of your own hearts. You will find it a bottomless pit. Examine the evidence of your interest in Christ, and labour to maintain sweet communion with

God. Make God your choice, and not your necessity. Labour to maintain such constant fellowship with him, that when you die, you only change your place, but not your company. Grow in the exercise of your graces (2 *Pet.* 1:5-7). Study to know God more, and love him better. Mind the one necessary thing—the Lord Jesus Christ, there are many maybe's, but only one must-be. Study the sufferings of Christ. Resolve with Paul to know nothing but Jesus Christ, and him crucified. A due contemplation of the cross will heighten Christ's love, and lessen your own sufferings. Labour to seek those things in heaven, looking for the coming of Christ (2 *Pet.* 3:12): Say, 'Come, Lord Jesus, come quickly.' Study thoroughly the sinfulness of sin, the emptiness of the earthly, and the fullness of Christ.

In all these, and like lessons, labour for an inward, convincing, experimental, powerful, sweet, abiding teaching. Do not rest in mere notions. Improve your time well in the school of the word. Labour to be instructed by the chastisements you see upon other men. Short work! Other's punishment is our caution. God did not spare the nations that he might tender his mercy on Israel. Severity to the nations, but goodness towards Israel! When the father is correcting one child, the whole family should fear and tremble. If we could learn by other men's suffering, we should prevent our own!

(2.) *To those who lie under affliction: Take notice, O afflicted soul, what God's design is in afflicting you, and make it your design— namely, that you might be taught, and that correction may be turned into instruction. Hear the rod, and who has appointed it.*

It is the great mistake and folly of men that they make more haste to get their afflictions removed than sanctified. Learning our lesson is the shortest way to deliverance. This is God's method. He teaches his people, and they will then not wait long for their deliverance.

Remember that God's design is to teach you. Blessings are not found in mere deliverance alone. It is a sad thing to feel the wood of the cross, but not the good of the cross; to taste the bitter root, but not the sweet fruit of a suffering condition; the curse, but not the cordial. Therefore mind instruction, study the lessons of a suffering condition. He chastens us for our profit, that we might be partakers of his holiness (*Heb.* 12:10).

(3.) *To those who have just come out of affliction and fiery trials: Reflect upon yourself, examine your heart.*

Were your afflictions accompanied by instruction? Has the rod budded? What have you learned? Have you learned the sinfulness of sin, the emptiness of creation, and the fullness of Christ? Have you learned that there is no evil like the evil of sin? Have you learned that there is no good like Jesus Christ? Has the world become empty in your eyes? Can you say, 'It is good I have been afflicted?' Do you know divine truth more inwardly, more clearly, more experimentally, more powerfully, more sweetly than ever? Does it have a more abiding impression upon your heart?

If you have come out of affliction without apparent divine teaching, and felt the blows of God but that is all; roll yourselves

in the dust before the Lord. Humble yourself greatly before him, and wrestle mightily
after the teaching of God upon your heart.
Say, 'Lord, you have given your servant
great deliverance from danger and death,
and shall I now perish for lack of teaching,
and go down to hell among the uncircum-
cised? "Teach me your way, O Lord, I will
walk in your truth. Unite my heart to fear
your name" (*Psa.* 86:11). Teach me to do
your will, for you are my God. Your Spirit is
good, lead me into the land of uprightness.'
In a word, desire the Lord that he would do
all the work, and then take all the glory. Say,
'Lord, teach me as well as deliver me, and I
shall be blessed.'

If by God's grace you have found the
fruit of affliction savoury and saving upon
your heart, let me commend a threefold
duty to you:

(i.) *Study to be thankful*. If God has taught you as well as chastised you, O say with David, 'What shall I render to the LORD?'

Consider what great things God has done for your soul. God has done more for you than if he had never brought you into affliction and trouble; more than if he had brought you out the same day that you went into trouble. If he had delivered you at your first prayer it would not have been as great a mercy as to teach you in your afflictions. Prevention and deliverance may be in wrath, but God never teaches the soul but in his love. God has doubled his mercy and lovingkindness to you and given deliverance and instruction too! This is a multiplied mercy that should greatly endear the heart to God and make it sing with David, 'I will love the LORD, because

he has heard the voice of my supplication'
(*Psa.* 116:1).

Upon the return of prayer in a single
deliverance, God expects the return of
praise: 'Call upon me in the day of trouble,
and I will deliver you, and you shall glorify
me' (*Psa.* 50:15). How much more should
we be grateful when the Lord twists his
mercies one in another! When he doubles
and triples and multiplies his mercy, we
should double and triple and multiply our
thankfulness. When God loads us with
mercy we should load him with our praises.

Behold, O Christian soul, God has
done for you in your sufferings that which
he possibly denied you in your prosperity.
It is a proof of your sonship. Your suffering time was your sealing time. He allured
you and brought you into the wilderness,

and there has spoken comfortably to your heart. Your Patmos has been your paradise in which he has given you his love.

God has consecrated your sufferings by his teaching. You have become a partaker of the divine nature (*2 Pet.* 1:4). Your soul now resembles God, holy as he is holy. God has changed the very nature of affliction; he has turned your water into wine; a prison, a bed of sickness, into a school, into a temple in which he has taught you that you share his image. Christ is not full until all his members have their measure of sufferings (*Col.* 1:24).

Glorify God then with your lips. Let the lips of prayer be turned into the tongue of praise. Tell what great things God has done for you. Extol him in psalms of thanksgiving. Also glorify God with your life. Live his praise. Go and put the lessons you have learned in print. 'Let your light so shine before men that they may see your good works and glorify your Father which is in heaven' (*Matt.* 5:16). Now that God has taught you, be ready to teach others. Communicate what God has taught you. 'Freely you have received, freely give.' God never lit this candle that it should be put under the bed or under the bushel.

(ii.) *Labour to preserve the teaching of God upon your spirit.* Study how to maintain that sweet gracious frame of heart that God has taught you by affliction. Look to yourselves that you do not lose the things that God has wrought in you.

(a.) *Often review the lessons you have been taught.* Take pains to keep the teachings of God alive in your spirits. Be sure of this that you will find a great difference between your hearts under affliction than when it is removed.

Without infinite watchfulness your hearts will be too hard for you. It is sad, and a wonder to consider, how a corruption will lie as if it were quite dead while danger and death are before us, and how suddenly and powerfully it will revive and betray the soul when the danger is over. We should hearken to the whisperings of lust in our own hearts and labour to suppress them; to crush the serpent while it is in the shell. If there are any floatings of sin in the imagination, while yet in prison, consider what force it will yield when at liberty and temptation and opportunities arise. Therefore keep watch over your heart with diligence. The Hebrew phrases it: 'In all your keep-ings keep your heart, for out of them come the issues of life.'

And when the days of affliction and trouble are gone, work the truths and counsels you have received frequently and fixedly upon your conscience. Always be in readiness to oppose and check temptation and practise every lesson that God has taught you.

(b.) *Renew often upon your soul the remembrance of the sharpness and bitterness of the affliction.* This will be a notable corrective to sensuality, and give check to sinful excesses. The flesh will quickly grow strong when it finds itself at ease. When you have come out of the house of bondage, remember the sorrows of a suffering condition. Do not set your heart so much upon the pleasure of your present enlargement, as upon the bitterness of your former captivity. Remembrance of former dispensations give good hope through grace.

(c.) *Call often to your mind the sad discourses and reasonings, the fears and tremblings that you have had in your heart in the times of trouble and distress.* When the waters flowed over your head and you began to sink in the mire, remember how your heart began to sink with fear. Recount the impatience, the murmur and unbelief, the love of a present world, the fear of death, the hard thoughts of God. Doubtless it would be of good use to humble your souls, to check corruption, and to endear and preserve the teachings of God upon your souls.

(d.) *Remember also your vows.* When God by the fire of affliction showed you your folly, and revealed the hidden corruption of your hearts, you vowed, 'I will do so no more.' Take heed you are not like backsliding Israel. This is the temper of our hearts. We are very good while we are in affliction, and promise fair; but no sooner is the trial over, we forget God's teachings and our own vows and return into the same course as before. Now if you would preserve the teachings of God upon your spirits, sit down, remember your vows and spreading them before the Lord, say with David, 'I will pay you my vows which my lips have uttered and my mouth has spoken when I was in trouble' (*Psa.* 66:13-14). Lord, through grace assisting, I will be ready to pay my vows, now I am well, as I was to make vows when I was sick!

(e.) *If you would preserve the teaching of God upon your heart, attend constantly upon the ministry of the word.* The truth is, the word and the rod teach the same lessons. The rod many times reminds us of the word. It quickens the word, and the word sanctifies the teachings of the rod. These mutually help to set one another with deeper impressions. The rod repeats the word, and the word repeats the instruction of the rod. The gospel will bring to remembrance what you have learned in the school of affliction.

(f.) *Often feed the frame of heart that God has taught you.* Give it day by day its daily bread. Seek meditations suitable to the nature of the grace you would like to maintain. Take heed of feeding corruption with thoughts of the sweetness that is in sin. Meditate much upon the sinfulness of sin, the emptiness of the creature, the fullness of Christ, to blessings of sufferings, the severity of the last judgment, the torments of hell, the joys of heaven, the infinite perfections of the divine nature, and the horror of eternity. Being rich in meditation brings richness in grace.

(g.) *Be much in prayer.* Stability only comes from the unchangeable God; therefore pray that God would put his unchangeableness upon you. O be earnest with God for stability of heart that your goodness may not be as the morning cloud, and as the early dew, but that it may resemble the Author of it, and be yesterday, and today, and for ever the same (*Heb.* 13:8). Confirm, O Lord in us what you have wrought, and perfect the work you have begun to your glory.

In a word, by all these means and

helps, labour Christians, to be such out of your afflictions, as you promised God and yourselves to be when you were in your afflictions.

(iii.) *Pray for the afflicted.* Pray for the Lord to teach them in their affliction that they may be blessed. Pray thus for all your friends who are, or have been in the furnace of affliction. Pray that they may come forth as gold purified seven times in the fire, that they may lose nothing there but their rust or dross. Pray, 'Lord, what they do not see, teach them, and if they have done wickedly, let them do so no more.' One great use that Christians should use of the scripture is to learn the language of prayer. O that Christians would learn how to pray for their brethren in tribulation; that they would censure less, and pray more. Instead of speaking of one another, speak more for one another. Show ourselves Christians indeed, not professors of the letter but of the spirit. We would gain our brethren instead of blasting them.

OTHER BOOKS IN THE
POCKET PURITANS
SERIES

Am I a Christian? James Fraser of Brea
Anger Management Richard Baxter
Binge Drinking John Flavel
Heaven, a World of Love Jonathan Edwards
Impure Lust John Flavel
Living Faith Samuel Ward
The Loveliness of Christ Samuel Rutherford (gift ed.)
Repent and Believe! Thomas Brooks
Sinful Speech John Flavel
Truth For All Time John Calvin (gift ed.)
The Westminster Shorter Catechism (booklet)
United We Stand Thomas Brooks

Richard Rushing has also edited
and made easy to read the following books by
John Owen:

The Mortification of Sin
ISBN: 978 0 85151 867 1
144pp. Paperback

Temptation: Resisted and Repulsed
ISBN: 978 0 85151 947 0
128pp. Paperback

For more details of all Banner of Truth titles,
please visit our website:
www.banneroftruth.co.uk

THE BANNER OF TRUTH TRUST

3 Murrayfield Road   P O Box 621, Carlisle
Edinburgh EH12 6EL   PA 17013
UK   USA

www.banneroftruth.co.uk